EMMANUEL JOSEPH

The Infinite Game, How Education and Gaming Can Lead to Spiritual Fulfillment

Copyright © 2025 by Emmanuel Joseph

All rights reserved. No part of this publication may be reproduced, stored or transmitted in any form or by any means, electronic, mechanical, photocopying, recording, scanning, or otherwise without written permission from the publisher. It is illegal to copy this book, post it to a website, or distribute it by any other means without permission.

First edition

*This book was professionally typeset on Reedsy.
Find out more at reedsy.com*

Contents

1   Chapter 1: The Nexus of Knowledge and Play   1
2   Chapter 2: The Evolution of Gaming in Education   3
3   Chapter 3: The Psychology of Play and Learning   5
4   Chapter 4: The Spiritual Dimension of Gaming   7
5   Chapter 5: The Role of Narrative in Games and Education   9
6   Chapter 6: The Impact of Gamification on Motivation   11
7   Chapter 7: The Role of Collaboration in Gaming and Education   13
8   Chapter 8: The Power of Simulation and Experiential Learning   15
9   Chapter 9: The Role of Reflection in Gaming and Education   17
10   Chapter 10: The Impact of Gaming on Emotional Intelligence   19
11   Chapter 11: The Intersection of Gaming and Mindfulness   21
12   Chapter 12: The Future of Education and Gaming   23
13   Chapter 13: The Role of Ethics in Gaming and Education   25
14   Chapter 14: The Intersection of Creativity and Gaming   27
15   Chapter 15: The Journey to Spiritual Fulfillment   29

1

Chapter 1: The Nexus of Knowledge and Play

In the world of education, gaming is often viewed as a distraction. However, this couldn't be further from the truth. When we explore the intricate relationship between gaming and education, we find that games can serve as powerful tools for learning. They provide an engaging platform for problem-solving, strategic thinking, and creativity, which are essential skills in any educational setting. Through the lens of gaming, education becomes a dynamic and interactive experience, fostering a deeper understanding of complex concepts.

Games have the unique ability to immerse players in alternative worlds, where they can experiment with different scenarios without real-world consequences. This freedom to explore and make mistakes is crucial for effective learning. It allows students to develop resilience and adaptability, as they learn from their failures and strive to improve. In this sense, gaming can be seen as a form of experiential learning, where players gain knowledge through hands-on experience.

Moreover, the social aspect of gaming cannot be overlooked. Many games require players to work together to achieve common goals, promoting teamwork and communication. These cooperative experiences can translate into valuable life skills, as individuals learn to collaborate and support each other. In an educational context, this can lead to a more inclusive and supportive learning environment, where students feel connected and motivated to succeed.

Ultimately, the nexus of knowledge and play is where the magic happens. When education and gaming intersect, they create a fertile ground for personal growth and development. By embracing the potential of games as educational tools, we can unlock new pathways to knowledge and understanding, leading to a more fulfilling and enriching learning experience.

2

Chapter 2: The Evolution of Gaming in Education

The integration of gaming into education is not a new concept, but it has evolved significantly over the years. Early educational games were often simplistic and focused on rote memorization, with limited interactivity. However, as technology has advanced, so too have the possibilities for gaming in education. Today's games offer sophisticated simulations and immersive experiences that can rival traditional teaching methods in effectiveness and engagement.

One of the most significant advancements in educational gaming is the use of gamification. This approach involves applying game design elements, such as point systems, leaderboards, and rewards, to non-game contexts. In education, gamification can motivate students to participate actively in their learning, as they strive to achieve higher scores and unlock new levels. This sense of progression and accomplishment can make learning more enjoyable and rewarding.

Another important development is the rise of educational virtual reality (VR) and augmented reality (AR) games. These technologies create immersive environments where students can interact with digital content in a three-dimensional space. For example, VR can transport students to historical sites, allowing them to explore ancient civilizations firsthand. AR can overlay digital information onto the real world, enhancing the learning experience with interactive elements. These innovations have the potential to revolutionize education, making it more engaging and accessible.

As gaming continues to evolve, so too will its role in education. The future promises even more exciting possibilities, as advancements in artificial intelligence, machine learning, and data analytics are incorporated into educational games. These technologies can provide personalized learning experiences tailored to each student's needs and abilities. By staying at the forefront of these developments, we can ensure that gaming remains a powerful and transformative force in education.

3

Chapter 3: The Psychology of Play and Learning

The psychology behind why we play games and how we learn is deeply intertwined. Games tap into our innate desire for exploration, mastery, and achievement. They provide a safe space for experimentation, where we can take risks and learn from our mistakes without fear of real-world consequences. This freedom to fail and try again is a crucial aspect of effective learning, as it encourages resilience and perseverance.

One of the key psychological principles at play in gaming is the concept of flow. Flow is a state of complete immersion and focus, where time seems to disappear, and individuals are fully engaged in the task at hand. Games are particularly adept at inducing flow, as they often require players to balance challenge and skill. When the difficulty level is just right, players enter a state of flow, where they are motivated to push their boundaries and achieve their goals. This same principle can be applied to education, where creating a challenging yet achievable learning environment can foster deep engagement and motivation.

Another important psychological factor is the sense of autonomy and control that games provide. Players have the freedom to make choices and influence the outcome of the game, which can lead to a sense of empowerment and agency. In an educational context, giving students more control over their learning can increase their intrinsic motivation and drive. By incorporating elements of choice and self-directed learning, educators can create a more personalized and engaging experience for their students.

The social aspect of gaming also plays a significant role in its psychological impact. Many games involve collaboration and competition, which can foster a sense of community and belonging. These social connections can enhance the learning experience, as students support and challenge each other to improve. By understanding the psychological principles behind play and learning, we can harness the power of games to create more effective and fulfilling educational experiences.

4

Chapter 4: The Spiritual Dimension of Gaming

Gaming is often seen as a purely recreational activity, but it can also have profound spiritual implications. At its core, gaming is about exploration and discovery, both of external worlds and of oneself. By engaging with games, individuals can embark on a journey of self-discovery and personal growth, which can lead to a deeper sense of spiritual fulfillment.

One way that gaming can contribute to spiritual growth is by providing a space for reflection and introspection. Many games feature complex narratives and moral dilemmas, which can prompt players to think deeply about their values and beliefs. By grappling with these issues in a virtual environment, players can gain new insights and perspectives that can inform their real-world actions and decisions.

Additionally, the immersive nature of games can create a sense of transcendence and connection to something greater than oneself. When players are fully absorbed in a game, they may experience a state of flow, where they feel a deep sense of unity and harmony with the game world. This feeling of oneness can be a powerful and transformative experience, akin to the spiritual experiences described in various religious and philosophical traditions.

Furthermore, the collaborative aspects of gaming can foster a sense of community and belonging, which is an essential component of spiritual fulfillment. Many games require players to work together to achieve common goals, promoting empathy, cooperation, and mutual support. These social connections can provide a sense of purpose and meaning, as individuals come together to create something greater than themselves.

In conclusion, gaming can be a powerful tool for spiritual growth and fulfillment. By providing opportunities for reflection, connection, and personal growth, games can help individuals discover deeper meanings and purposes in their lives. By embracing the spiritual dimension of gaming, we can unlock new pathways to self-discovery and enlightenment.

5

Chapter 5: The Role of Narrative in Games and Education

Narrative plays a crucial role in both games and education, as it provides a framework for understanding and interpreting experiences. In games, narrative can create a compelling context for gameplay, drawing players into the game world and motivating them to engage with the content. Similarly, in education, narrative can help students make sense of complex concepts and ideas, by connecting them to relatable stories and experiences.

Games are particularly adept at using narrative to enhance the learning experience. Many games feature rich and immersive storylines, which can captivate players' imaginations and keep them engaged. By weaving educational content into these narratives, games can make learning more enjoyable and meaningful. For example, historical games can transport players to different time periods, allowing them to experience history firsthand and develop a deeper understanding of historical events and figures.

In an educational context, narrative can also be a powerful tool for fostering critical thinking and creativity. By encouraging students to create their own stories and scenarios, educators can help them develop their imagination and problem-solving skills. This can be achieved through various activities, such as creative writing, role-playing, and storytelling. By integrating narrative into the learning process, educators can create a more dynamic and engaging experience for their students.

Furthermore, narrative can help to build empathy and emotional intelligence, which are essential components of spiritual fulfillment. By engaging with different characters and perspectives in games and stories, individuals can develop a deeper understanding of others' experiences and emotions. This can foster a sense of compassion and connection, which can enrich their personal and spiritual lives.

In conclusion, narrative is a powerful tool for both games and education. By leveraging the power of stories, we can create more engaging and meaningful learning experiences that foster personal growth and spiritual fulfillment. Through the lens of narrative, we can unlock new pathways to knowledge and understanding, and inspire individuals to explore the infinite possibilities of their own potential.

6

Chapter 6: The Impact of Gamification on Motivation

G amification, the application of game design elements to non-game contexts, has gained significant attention in recent years for its potential to enhance motivation and engagement. In education, gamification can transform traditional learning environments by making them more interactive and rewarding. By incorporating elements such as points, badges, and leaderboards, educators can create a sense of competition and achievement that motivates students to participate actively in their learning.

One of the key benefits of gamification is its ability to provide immediate feedback and recognition. In a gamified learning environment, students receive instant feedback on their performance, which can help them identify areas for improvement and build confidence in their abilities. This continuous cycle of feedback and recognition can create a positive reinforcement loop, where students are motivated to keep striving for success.

Additionally, gamification can foster a sense of autonomy and control, which is crucial for intrinsic motivation. By giving students the freedom to make choices and set their own goals, educators can create a more personalized and engaging learning experience. This sense of ownership and agency can empower students to take an active role in their education and pursue their interests with greater enthusiasm.

Gamification can also enhance motivation by creating a sense of community and collaboration. Many gamified learning environments incorporate social elements, such as team challenges and group projects, which encourage students to work together and support each other. This sense of camaraderie and shared purpose can foster a positive and inclusive learning environment, where students feel connected and motivated to succeed.

Moreover, gamification can make learning more enjoyable and engaging by tapping into the elements that make games fun. By incorporating game-like features such as quests, missions, and challenges, educators can create a more dynamic and interactive learning experience. This can help to alleviate the monotony of traditional learning methods and keep students engaged and motivated.

In conclusion, gamification has the potential to revolutionize education by enhancing motivation and engagement. By applying game design elements to the learning process, we can create a more interactive and rewarding experience that motivates students to participate actively in their education. This can lead to a deeper and more meaningful learning experience, fostering personal growth and spiritual fulfillment.

7

Chapter 7: The Role of Collaboration in Gaming and Education

Collaboration is a fundamental aspect of both gaming and education, as it promotes teamwork, communication, and mutual support. In many games, players must work together to achieve common goals, which can foster a sense of community and shared purpose. This collaborative spirit can translate into valuable life skills, as individuals learn to collaborate and support each other in their personal and professional lives.

In an educational context, collaboration can enhance the learning experience by encouraging students to share their knowledge and perspectives. Group projects, team challenges, and peer review activities can provide opportunities for students to work together and learn from each other. This can foster a more inclusive and supportive learning environment, where students feel valued and motivated to succeed.

The collaborative nature of games can also help to build empathy and understanding, as players work together to overcome challenges and achieve their goals. By experiencing different perspectives and learning to cooperate with others, individuals can develop a deeper sense of empathy and compassion. This can enrich their personal and spiritual lives, as they learn to connect with others on a deeper level.

In conclusion, collaboration is a powerful tool for both gaming and education. By fostering teamwork, communication, and mutual support, we can create a more inclusive and enriching learning experience. This can lead to personal growth and spiritual fulfillment, as individuals learn to connect and collaborate with others in meaningful ways.

8

Chapter 8: The Power of Simulation and Experiential Learning

Simulation and experiential learning are powerful tools for education, as they provide hands-on experience and practical application of knowledge. Games are particularly adept at creating realistic simulations, where players can experiment with different scenarios and learn from their experiences. This can make learning more engaging and meaningful, as students gain a deeper understanding of complex concepts through direct experience.

One of the key benefits of simulation and experiential learning is the ability to make mistakes and learn from them in a safe environment. In a game, players can take risks and try different approaches without real-world consequences. This freedom to fail and try again is crucial for effective learning, as it encourages resilience and perseverance. In an educational context, simulations can provide valuable opportunities for students to practice and refine their skills in a controlled environment.

Another important aspect of simulation and experiential learning is the development of critical thinking and problem-solving skills. By engaging with realistic scenarios, students are challenged to think creatively and strategically, as they work to overcome obstacles and achieve their goals. This can foster a deeper understanding of the subject matter and enhance their ability to apply their knowledge in real-world situations.

In conclusion, simulation and experiential learning are powerful tools for education, as they provide hands-on experience and practical application of knowledge. By leveraging the power of games, we can create more engaging and meaningful learning experiences that foster personal growth and spiritual fulfillment. Through the lens of simulation and experiential learning, we can unlock new pathways to knowledge and understanding.

9

Chapter 9: The Role of Reflection in Gaming and Education

Reflection is a crucial component of both gaming and education, as it provides an opportunity for individuals to process and internalize their experiences. In games, players often engage in reflective thinking as they analyze their strategies, learn from their mistakes, and plan their next moves. This reflective process can lead to a deeper understanding of the game mechanics and a greater sense of mastery and achievement.

In an educational context, reflection can enhance the learning experience by encouraging students to think critically about their progress and growth. Reflective activities, such as journaling, self-assessment, and group discussions, can provide valuable opportunities for students to analyze their learning and identify areas for improvement. This can foster a deeper sense of self-awareness and personal growth, as students learn to take ownership of their learning journey.

The reflective nature of gaming can also contribute to spiritual growth and fulfillment, as individuals contemplate their values, beliefs, and goals. By engaging in reflective thinking, players can gain new insights and perspectives that can inform their real-world actions and decisions. This can lead to a deeper sense of purpose and meaning, as individuals strive to align their actions with their values and beliefs.

In conclusion, reflection is a powerful tool for both gaming and education, as it provides an opportunity for individuals to process and internalize their experiences. By incorporating reflective activities into the learning process, we can create a more meaningful and enriching experience that fosters personal growth and spiritual fulfillment. Through the lens of reflection, we can gain new insights and perspectives, and unlock the infinite possibilities of our own potential.

10

Chapter 10: The Impact of Gaming on Emotional Intelligence

G aming can have a significant impact on emotional intelligence, as it provides opportunities for individuals to develop their self-awareness, empathy, and social skills. Many games require players to navigate complex social dynamics, manage their emotions, and understand the perspectives of others. This can foster a deeper sense of emotional intelligence, as individuals learn to recognize and regulate their emotions and develop healthy relationships with others.

One of the key benefits of gaming is the ability to practice emotional regulation in a controlled environment. In a game, players may experience a range of emotions, from excitement and joy to frustration and disappointment. By learning to manage these emotions and maintain focus, players can develop valuable coping skills that can be applied to real-world situations.

Additionally, the social aspect of gaming can enhance empathy and social skills, as players interact with others and navigate different perspectives and experiences. Cooperative games, in particular, require players to work together and support each other, fostering a sense of teamwork and mutual understanding. This can lead to a greater sense of community and connection, as individuals learn to appreciate the diverse perspectives and experiences of others.

In conclusion, gaming can have a profound impact on emotional intelligence, as it provides opportunities for individuals to develop their self-awareness, empathy, and social skills. By leveraging the power of games, we can create more enriching and meaningful experiences that foster personal growth and spiritual fulfillment. Through the lens of gaming, we can unlock new pathways to emotional intelligence and connect with others on a deeper level.

11

Chapter 11: The Intersection of Gaming and Mindfulness

Mindfulness, the practice of being present and fully engaged in the moment, can be a powerful tool for personal growth and spiritual fulfillment. In the context of gaming, mindfulness can enhance the experience by helping players stay focused, manage their emotions, and fully immerse themselves in the game world. By practicing mindfulness, players can develop a deeper sense of self-awareness and presence, which can enrich their gaming experience and their overall well-being.

One way that mindfulness can be incorporated into gaming is through mindful play, where players consciously focus on their actions, thoughts, and emotions while playing. This can help players stay present and engaged, reducing distractions and enhancing their enjoyment of the game. Additionally, mindful play can promote emotional regulation and stress management, as players learn to recognize and manage their emotions in a healthy and constructive way.

Another important aspect of mindfulness in gaming is the concept of flow, a state of complete immersion and focus where individuals are fully engaged in the task at hand. Games are particularly adept at inducing flow, as they often require players to balance challenge and skill. By practicing mindfulness, players can enter a state of flow more easily and maintain it for longer periods, enhancing their gaming experience and their overall well-being.

In conclusion, the intersection of gaming and mindfulness can create powerful opportunities for personal growth and spiritual fulfillment. By incorporating mindfulness practices into the gaming experience, players can develop a deeper sense of self-awareness, presence, and emotional regulation. This can lead to a more enriching and meaningful experience, both in gaming and in life.

12

Chapter 12: The Future of Education and Gaming

As we look to the future, the potential for education and gaming to intersect and transform the learning experience is vast. With advancements in technology, such as virtual reality, augmented reality, and artificial intelligence, the possibilities for creating immersive and personalized learning experiences are expanding. By embracing these innovations, we can create more engaging and meaningful educational environments that foster personal growth and spiritual fulfillment.

One of the key trends in the future of education and gaming is the rise of personalized learning, where educational content and experiences are tailored to the individual needs and preferences of each student. Through the use of data analytics and machine learning, educators can create customized learning pathways that optimize each student's progress and engagement. This can lead to more effective and enjoyable learning experiences, as students receive the support and resources they need to succeed.

Another important trend is the increasing focus on experiential and project-based learning, where students engage in hands-on activities and real-world projects. Games and simulations can play a crucial role in this approach, providing realistic scenarios and challenges that allow students to apply their knowledge and skills in a practical context. This can enhance the learning experience and prepare students for success in their future careers and personal lives.

In conclusion, the future of education and gaming holds immense potential for creating more engaging and meaningful learning experiences. By embracing the power of games and technology, we can transform the learning process and foster personal growth and spiritual fulfillment. Through the lens of education and

13

Chapter 13: The Role of Ethics in Gaming and Education

Ethics plays a crucial role in both gaming and education, as it guides individuals in making responsible and moral decisions. In games, ethical dilemmas often arise, challenging players to consider the consequences of their actions and make choices that align with their values. By grappling with these issues in a virtual environment, players can develop a deeper understanding of ethics and morality, which can inform their real-world behavior.

In an educational context, ethics can be integrated into the curriculum through discussions, case studies, and experiential learning activities. By examining ethical issues and dilemmas, students can develop critical thinking skills and learn to navigate complex moral landscapes. This can foster a sense of responsibility and integrity, as individuals learn to consider the impact of their actions on others and the world around them.

The ethical dimension of gaming can also contribute to personal and spiritual growth, as individuals reflect on their values and beliefs. By engaging with ethical dilemmas in games, players can gain new insights and perspectives that can inform their real-world actions and decisions. This can lead to a deeper sense of purpose and meaning, as individuals strive to align their actions with their values and beliefs.

In conclusion, ethics is a powerful tool for both gaming and education, as it guides individuals in making responsible and moral decisions. By incorporating ethical discussions and activities into the learning process, we can create a more meaningful and enriching experience that fosters personal growth and spiritual fulfillment. Through the lens of ethics, we can gain new insights and perspectives, and unlock the infinite possibilities of our own potential.

14

Chapter 14: The Intersection of Creativity and Gaming

Creativity is a fundamental aspect of both gaming and education, as it fosters innovation, problem-solving, and self-expression. In games, creativity is often required to overcome challenges, develop strategies, and create new content. By engaging with games, individuals can develop their creative thinking skills and explore new possibilities.

In an educational context, creativity can be nurtured through various activities, such as art, music, writing, and design. By encouraging students to express themselves and think outside the box, educators can create a more dynamic and engaging learning experience. This can foster a sense of curiosity and exploration, as students are motivated to discover new ideas and solutions.

The creative nature of gaming can also contribute to personal and spiritual growth, as individuals explore their passions and interests. By engaging in creative activities, players can develop a deeper sense of self-awareness and self-expression. This can lead to a greater sense of fulfillment and purpose, as individuals discover their unique talents and abilities.

In conclusion, creativity is a powerful tool for both gaming and education, as it fosters innovation, problem solving, and self-expression. By nurturing creativity, we can create a more dynamic and engaging learning experience that fosters personal growth and spiritual fulfillment. Through the lens of creativity, we can unlock new pathways to knowledge and understanding, and inspire individuals to explore the infinite possibilities of their own potential.

15

Chapter 15: The Journey to Spiritual Fulfillment

The journey to spiritual fulfillment is a deeply personal and unique experience for each individual. It involves exploring one's values, beliefs, and purpose, and finding ways to align one's actions with these principles. In the context of gaming and education, this journey can be enriched by the opportunities for reflection, connection, and personal growth that these activities provide.

By engaging with games and educational experiences, individuals can embark on a journey of self-discovery and personal growth. This journey may involve overcoming challenges, developing new skills, and gaining new insights and perspectives. Through this process, individuals can develop a deeper understanding of themselves and their place in the world.

The journey to spiritual fulfillment also involves connecting with others and fostering a sense of community and belonging. By working together and supporting each other, individuals can create meaningful connections and shared experiences that enrich their personal and spiritual lives. This sense of community can provide a source of strength and inspiration, as individuals strive to achieve their goals and fulfill their potential.

In conclusion, the journey to spiritual fulfillment is a deeply personal and unique experience that can be enriched by the opportunities for reflection, connection, and personal growth provided by gaming and education. By embracing these activities, individuals can explore their values, beliefs, and purpose, and find ways to align their actions with these principles. Through this journey, we can discover the infinite possibilities of our own potential and achieve a deeper sense of fulfillment and meaning in our lives.

The Infinite Game: How Education and Gaming Can Lead to Spiritual Fulfillment

In a world where the lines between reality and virtual worlds are increasingly blurred, "The Infinite Game" explores the profound connection between education, gaming, and spiritual fulfillment. This thought-provoking book delves into the ways in which the interactive and immersive nature of games can revolutionize traditional learning methods, fostering personal growth and a deeper sense of purpose.

Through twelve captivating chapters, readers are taken on a journey that reveals how gaming can enhance critical thinking, creativity, emotional intelligence, and collaboration. The book highlights the transformative power of gamification and experiential learning, showcasing how these approaches can make education more engaging and meaningful.

At its core, "The Infinite Game" is about the spiritual dimension of gaming. It explores how games can provide opportunities for reflection, self-discovery, and connection with others. By embracing the potential of games as tools for personal and spiritual growth, readers can unlock new pathways to fulfillment and enlightenment.

Whether you are an educator, a gamer, or someone seeking a deeper understanding of the role of play in our lives, "The Infinite Game" offers valuable insights and practical guidance. This book invites you to explore the infinite possibilities of your own potential and discover how the intersection of education and gaming can lead to a richer, more fulfilling life.

www.ingramcontent.com/pod-product-compliance
Lightning Source LLC
LaVergne TN
LVHW010443070526
838199LV00066B/6172